NO MORE SILENCE

There Is Safety

NO MORE SILENCE

There Is Safety

Dr. Teresa Woods, D. Min., LMSW

Copyright © 2019 by Dr. Teresa Woods
Published by Glimpse of Glory Christian Book Publishing
ISBN: 978-0-9983588-2-6

Printed in the United States of America

Unless otherwise noted Scriptures are taken from King James Version Bible and the Message Bible.

All rights reserved. No part of this publication may be reproduced, stored in a retrieval system or transmitted, in any form, or by any means, electronic, mechanical, recorded, photocopied, or otherwise, without the prior permission of the copyright owner, except by a reviewer who may quote brief passages in a review.

CONTENTS

ACKNOWLEDGMENTS 7

INTRODUCTION 9

CHAPTER ONE: HOW DID WE GET HERE? 13

CHAPTER TWO: THE TWO SHALL NOT BE IGNORED ... 27

CHAPTER THREE: MENTAL ILLNESS; WHY IS THE CHURCH SILENT?... 37

CHAPTER FOUR: THERE IS SAFETY BECAUSE THERE IS HELP 49

THOUGHT PROVOKING QUESTIONS 59

JOURNAL 63

ABOUT THE AUTHOR 89

ACKNOWLEDGMENTS

To my dissertation committee:
This book would not have been written if the topic had not pierced my heart so deeply as I was pondering a dissertation topic. Therefore, I am very appreciative of my dissertation committee at American Bible University and for their love and support shown during the loss of my mother.

To my late mother:

This book is dedicated to my late mother who was my greatest inspiration and supporter. Every step I make, I keep Jesus on my mind and you in my heart.

INTRODUCTION

According to the United States Department of Health and Human Services (2016), mental health includes our emotional, psychological, and social well-being. It affects how we think, feel, and act. It also determines how we handle stress, relate to others, and make choices. Mental health is important at every stage of life from childhood to adolescence to adulthood. Therefore, it is each individual's responsibility to do what is needed to protect it and ensure their holistic well-being.

Mental health has been a concern and mental illness has existed in the church since biblical times. There is a story about a young man who continued to throw himself into the fire even after his family did everything they knew to do to help him (Mark 9:22 KJV). It was concluded that he was possessed by a demon and after the demon was cast out, the young man was made whole (vv.22-29, KJV). We read of another instance where one of Jesus' disciples, Judas became so depressed after betraying Jesus that he was the cause of his own death (Matthew 27:5, KJV). At some point, everyone will experience some type of mental health issue. The most common are anxiety, depression, grief, and panic attacks (Feist & Rosenberg, 2014, p. 253).

Being in the field of social work for twenty years, providing therapy for sixteen years and a minister of the gospel for eight years, I have been privileged to see mental illness from the physical as well as the spiritual side. This book addresses the problem of American church leaders who are not trained to address mental health issues such as depression and anxiety within their congregations. This problem exists primarily because it is not a requirement that church leaders be trained to address mental health issues within their congregations (Rainer, 2015). Some church leaders still believe that mental health is a private issue that should be addressed internally or by outside mental health professionals; while some believe that mental health is a spiritual issue that can only be resolved by the church. The research gap in literature shows that the American church and churches in general tend to underutilize mental health resources available to their congregations (Dempsey, Butler, & Gaither, 2015).

According to the National Alliance on Mental Illness (2017), serious mental illness costs America $193.2 billion in earnings a year with approximately 1 in 5 or about 43.8 million adults experiencing some type of mental illness in a given year. Approximately 1 in 5 youth aged 13-18 experience a severe mental disorder at some point during their life. At least 16 million adults had at least one major depressive episode in the past year. These statistics note that most homeless adults living in shelters live with some type of mental illness and/or substance use disorders. Other special populations impacted by mental health issues are state prisoners and juvenile delinquents. African Americans use mental health services at one half the rate of Caucasians.

Today, most ministers connect depression to socio-economical issues like poverty, substance abuse, poor nutrition and financial instability to name a few. Feist & Rosenberg (2014) mention all are prevalent among the African American population. Therefore, church leaders are in favor of church-based mental health programs to address mental health issues in the African American congregation (Brown & Keith, 2013, p. 14). Church leaders also need to be aware of any state or local laws governing their practice of any church-based mental health programs. For example, in the State of Alabama, church leaders/clergy should adhere to both legal and ethical guidelines concerning confidentiality when providing counseling to the members of their church, just as some professionals do in their line of work. They are not to disclose any information unless the member has threatened to harm themselves or others. Also, there are mandated reporting laws in which church leaders are legally responsible for reporting allegations involving any form of abuse and/or neglect.

CHAPTER 1

How Did We Get Here?

Brief Overview of Mental Illness

The history of mental illness and treatment of mental illness dates back to 5000 B.C. Its origin surrounds ancient Greek and Roman writings (Farreras, 2017). For many, it was viewed as either a religious or a personal problem. In reference to the religious aspect, mental illness was looked upon by some as a type of demonic possession. Meaning, conditions that we now know as depression, schizophrenia, and/or bipolar disorder were known as some type of evil force which had taken over your life and caused you to react in strange ways and do strange things. The only treatment used was prayer and holy water. They were used together to cast out what was called evil spirits or demons. The treatment was successful if the mental illness left the body which was evident by the behavior changing or being eliminated altogether. Today, some people still believe in this phenomenon just like some believe that mental illness is more physical than spiritual.

The personal problem coincides with people believing that mental illness stems from trauma or conflict in a person's life. Meaning, the more problems you have, the more likely you are to experience some type of mental challenge. Some research shows that too much stress or pressure in a person's life can lead to a chemical imbalance in the brain which alters the behavior of a person. As a result, we see the surfacing of schizophrenia and other mental illnesses like bipolar disorder.

When this occurred, it was essential that the affected individual receive some type of treatment (Slate, Buffington-Vollum, & Johnson, 2013).

Supernatural, Somatogenic or Psychogenic?

Throughout history, there have been three general theories on the etiology of mental illness: (1) supernatural, (2) somatogenic, and (3) psychogenic. Supernatural theories attribute mental illness to curses, sin, and evil and demonic spirits (Dictionary.com). The curses could be spoken or written and where known to have supernatural powers. For example, if a person did not like you or wanted to cause problems for you, they would seek what was known as a spiritual advisor who would mix potions and speak curses in hopes of something happening to the target individual. Sometimes, the curses were written down and placed next to magic potions and other representational articles to target the individual. In biblical times, these curses were known as forms of witchcraft that needed to be avoided at all costs (Cockerham, 2016).

Throughout classical antiquity, there was a return to supernatural theories of demonic possession or godly displeasure to account for abnormal behavior that was beyond the person's control. Temple attendance with religious healing ceremonies and incantations to the gods were employed to assist in the healing process. Hebrews saw madness as punishment from God, so treatment consisted of confessing sins and repenting (Farreras, 2017). Certain religions, specifically Christianity associated sin with mental illness. If you were not keeping God's commandments then you were living in sin which made you subject to evil and demonic spirits taking over your body. Once these spirits take over the body, it opens you up to mental illness and all other forms of illness to include physical disparities. Sin is equated with anything bad and therefore, mental illness is considered as bad. If you had an evil or demonic spirit, it was also bad. However, the intent was on eliminating the sin along with the evil and demonic spirits in hopes of eliminating the mental illness (Islam & Campbell, 2014).

According to Santrock (2013), somatogenic theories identify disturbances in physical functioning resulting from either illness, genetics, brain damage or imbalance. Illness can impact our physical bodies in many ways. Some illnesses can lead to an inability to walk, see, or hear. For example, most individuals who have been diagnosed with diabetes normally experience issues with sight. These issues may lead to having cataracts removed or a surgical procedure for glaucoma. Other illness like scarlet fever and meningitis have left people paralyzed in some way if the illness did not physically kill them. Again, when a body is impacted physically, it can cause mental and emotional disturbances (Santrock, 2013).

Genetics has been connected to mental illness through research (Hall, 2013). If a parent suffers from some type of mental illness, it is likely that the child will experience some of the same problems. Recently, there was a made for television movie called "The Secret She Kept" (Glass & Others, 2016) in which a very well-known African American attorney suffered from both schizoaffective and bipolar disorder. It is revealed that the character Tia's father suffered from these symptoms and even one of the grandparents suffered from some of the same symptoms. They did not fully emerge to cause a breakdown until Tia launched a political campaign to run for office. These stressors overwhelmed her life and because she did not take her medications on a regular basis, the symptoms were uncontrolled and resurfaced wreaking havoc on her new marriage and her career. The family tried to keep matters quiet but eventually Tia came forward and shared with her supporters and other family members about her mental illness.

Brain damage in itself can cause an imbalance. We have heard of head injuries leading to amnesia and multiple personality disorders. Amnesia is the loss of one's memory from some type of physical or psychological trauma (Santrock, 2013). People have walked away from car accidents with amnesia. In the same respect, people may have witnessed someone else being murdered and walked away with amnesia from the psychological trauma. When the person cannot remember their identity, it can lead to giving themselves another identity and even after the original one returns, the alter ego may still exist. This is known as multiple personality disorder. Psychogenic theories focus on traumatic or stressful experiences, learned associations or distorted perceptions (Santrock, 2013). The term psycho is almost always associated with psychology and the mind in some way. Somewhere within our minds, we are very sensitive to external stimuli which may send our brains into overload. When this happens, the shift may take place and cause an imbalance to occur. Most scientists believe this imbalance is what leads to mental illness (Kemp, Lickel, & Deacon, 2014). Still, further research has to show how these mental illnesses developed and which ones are most commonly associated with stressful experiences, learned associations or distorted perceptions.

In 1756 and 1773, America established hospitals and asylums for the mentally ill. Two of the most well-known are the Pennsylvania Hospital in Philadelphia and the Williamsburg Hospital in Virginia. The Pennsylvania Hospital is the first American public institution that accepted the mentally ill for treatment and cure. It was also the first to show a humane approach to insanity. There were many hospitals in Europe and other countries which were specifically for the mentally ill.

However, it was not until Williamsburg Hospital in Virginia was established that there was now an asylum in America to treat only the mentally ill (Deutsch, 2013).

The father of American psychiatry, Benjamin Rush (1745-1813) promoted the somatogenic theory of mental illness that led to treatments like blood-letting and tranquilizer chairs (Pellegrini, 2010). After graduating from Princeton at the age of fifteen and completing his medical apprenticeship in Europe, Dr. Rush became a chemistry professor who was very interested in mental disease. Later, he joined the staff at Pennsylvania Hospital and served there for thirty years studying mental disorders and treating patients diagnosed with mental illnesses. Dr. Rush was the person who cut down the thick layers of association between superstition and mental illness. For the first time, the topic was raised to a scientific level (Deutsch, 2013).

Mental Illness aka "Madness"

When it comes to discussing the history of mental illness in America, initially, it was referred to as "madness". Madness implies that there is too much of something. The emergence of mental illness in America caused many to develop an uncertainty as to whether America was equipped to handle such an outbreak (Young, 2010). They questioned if control was possible and if so, who would be responsible for all those who were diagnosed as being mentally ill. When Pennsylvania had the only hospital to treat the mentally ill, they had to place everyone on one floor which was known as a psych ward. For many outsiders, they referred to it as the "lunatic floor". Many were thankful to see Williamsburg Hospital in Virginia which was built specifically to house those diagnosed as being mentally ill (Young, 2010).

The general population did not feel as if those with physical illnesses should be housed in the same hospital as the mentally ill. As we can see from earlier literature research, this marked a change in how mental illness was once seen as somatogenic or a physical problem to more of a psychogenic or supernatural issue. During the separation process, there was a development of asylums that took place. These asylums provided shelter, food, and a place of safety for those who were emotionally disturbed. With psychiatrists on staff like Dr. Rush, these patients received treatments that would stabilize them and if they maintained stabilization over an extended period of time, they were able to return to modern day society (Young, 2010).

Dr. James McCune Smith, the first black physician to practice medicine in the United States was also instrumental in this madness movement and the history of mental illness in America (Young, 2010). He along with Edward Jarvis analyzed the mentally ill census in the United States in 1844 to determine if there were erroneous errors when it came to the number of blacks who were reported as being mentally ill in comparison to the number of whites. The findings show that blacks were more prone to be enslaved to madness than whites. They were placed in hospitals and asylums more than whites and this had a lot to do with the slavery movement. Smith was one who fought to change things by reducing the census and helping more blacks to be free from the stigma attached to the mentally ill (Young, 2010).

In addition to Dr. Rush and Dr. Smith, Dorothea Dix was another great activist who contributed to the history of mental illness in America. Ms. Dix's concern was the living conditions for the mentally ill after witnessing dangerous and unhealthy conditions in which most patients lived. This concern led to much lobbying and after forty years of doing so, Dix was able to convince the United States government to provide funding for the building of thirty-two state psychiatric hospitals throughout the country (Unite for Sight, 2015). Having patients institutionalized for mental illness had some benefits for America. Two of them include: (1) psychiatric hospitals with professional staff were considered the most effective way to care for the mentally ill and (2) family members who were struggling to care for their mentally ill loved ones welcomed the placements. However, by the 1950's there was a push towards deinstitutionalization which simply means instead of a long-term stay in a psychiatric hospital, they preferred a less isolated community mental health setting (Unite for Sight, 2015). For example, community mental health centers or community nursing homes. This probably resulted from the need for the mentally ill to return to the community once their symptoms were under control and/or their condition had been stabilized.

In 1963, the Community Mental Health Act imposed strict standards on state psychiatric hospitals. Meaning, only persons who were considered an immediate danger to themselves or others were allowed to be placed in a psychiatric hospital setting. All others would receive outpatient treatment that stems from the move towards community oriented care (Sheffield, 2016). By the mid-1960's, America saw many severely mental ill people moved from psychiatric institutions to local community health homes or similar facilities. The number of institutionalized mentally ill experienced a dramatic decline from 560,000 patients in the 1950s to 130,000 patients by 1980. Also by the millennium, the number of state psychiatric hospital beds per 100,000 patients was 22 compared to 339 in 1950 (Sheffield, 2016).

The goal of deinstitutionalization was to improve treatment and the quality of life for the mentally ill. The other positives include the development of friendships, overall patient satisfaction, and a marked improvement in life skills and personal hygiene. Still, it appears as if the negatives may outweigh the positives. Studies show that since deinstitutionalization, many patients living in community type settings have significant deficits in health care matters such as vaccinations, cancer screenings, and routine medical checkups. There has been an increase in loneliness among the patients, poverty, poor health, and unsanitary living conditions. Deinstitutionalization shifted the care for the mentally ill back into the hands of the family opposed to trained professional staff. Many families lack the medical knowledge and/or financial resources they need to do an effective job (Unite for Sight, 2015).

Diagnosing Mental Illness

When it comes to diagnosing and treating mental illness, one of the most powerful tools used was developed in 1952, and is known as the Diagnostics for Statistical Manual of Mental Disorders (DSM). The first DSM came post World War II as a variant for the ICD-6. The DSM contains a glossary of descriptions of the diagnostic categories and was the first official manual of mental disorders to focus on clinical use. The DSM contains many revisions that resulted from an expansion of categories for classification of different types of mental illness. One revision, the DSM-III was published in 1980 (APA, 2017). It introduced a number of important advances, including specific diagnostic criteria, a multiaxial diagnostic assessment system, and an approach that attempted to be unbiased with respect to the causes of mental disorders. This revision was developed with an additional goal of providing detailed definitions of mental disorders for clinicians and researchers (APA, 2017).

The DSM-IV was published in 1994. This revision provided a comprehensive review of literature to establish a safe pragmatic basis for making modifications. Numerous changes were made to the classification, to the diagnostic criteria sets, and to the descriptive text (APA, 2017). There were new disorders added, some were deleted, while others were reorganized. The latest revision, DSM-V was published in 2013. Cohorts were fashioned to create a research agenda for this revision. These cohorts generated hundreds of white papers, profiles, and journal articles, providing the field with a summary on the state of the science and its relevance to psychiatric diagnoses. The DSM-V lets clinicians know the existing gaps in current research with hopes that more emphasis would be placed on research within those areas (APA, 2017).

Currently, 1 in 5 Americans are suffering from some type of mental illness. According to the National Trends in Mental Health Care, an average of 29 per 100 adults in 2010 were diagnosed with a mental disorder during an outpatient visit. As far as the youth is concerned or individuals who are less than 21 years of age, the average was 15 per 100 who were diagnosed with a mental disorder. 66 per 100 adults are taking psychotropic medications and 17 per 100 youth are taking psychotropic medications. What was surprising being that even though we have a number of adults and youth with mental disorders and taking psychotropic medications, not many are being seen for psychotherapy during outpatient treatment. Only 6 per 100 adults and 3 per 100 youth are being seen for psychotherapy or outpatient treatment (Olfson, Blanco, Wang, Laje, & Correll, 2017).

It is important to remember that 4 of the 10 leading causes of disabilities in America are mental disorders: (1) major depression, (2) schizophrenia, (3) bipolar disorder, and (4) obsessive compulsive disorder. It is also important to remember that people tend to suffer from more than one mental disorder at a time. This means that many may have a dual diagnosis such as bipolar and major depression or anxiety and panic attacks. These are some of the most notable ones that are found together. As stated earlier, all diagnoses are based upon information written in the DSM-V. For a person to be diagnosed with major depression, they must meet the following criteria; at least five or more of the following symptoms have to be available lasting for a two week period and at least one of the symptoms must be either a depressed mood or a loss of interest or pleasure: (1) depressed mood most of the day (feelings of sadness or hopelessness), (2) diminished interest or pleasure in all or almost all activities most of the day or every day, (3) significant weight loss when not dieting or weight gain or a decrease or increase in appetite nearly every day, (4) insomnia or hypersomnia every day, (5) psychomotor agitation (feelings of restlessness), (6) fatigue or loss of energy every day, (7) feelings of worthlessness or inappropriate guilt almost every day, (8) diminished ability to think or concentrate, or indecisiveness nearly every day, and (9) recurrent thoughts of death or suicidal ideation without a plan (DSM-V, 2013).

Schizophrenia is a brain disorder that affects how people think, feel, and perceive. The hallmark symptom of schizophrenia is psychosis such as auditory hallucinations (hearing voices) and delusions (false beliefs). The symptoms for schizophrenia fall into four domains: (1) positive symptoms-hallucinations and delusions, (2) negative symptoms-poverty of speech and loss of interests, (3) cognitive symptoms-memory deficits and difficulty understanding, and (4) mood symptoms-cheerful than sad or depressed mood. To meet the diagnostic criteria, the patient must experience at least two of the following: delusions, hallucinations, disorganized speech, disorganized or catatonic behavior, or negative symptoms. At least three of the symptoms mentioned on the list must be present. The disturbance must exist for 6 months and cannot be related to another condition (Frankenburg, 2017).

Major Depression and Schizophrenia are slightly different from Bipolar Disorder in that there are two things going on at the same time. Meaning, a bouncing around between manic episodes and depressive episodes. Bipolar disorder causes a variety of symptoms that can be very stressful and disruptive to a person's life and it is considered a chronic condition that affects the brain. It was formerly called manic-depressive illness (Frankenburg, 2017). The condition causes ups and downs in mood, behavior, energy, and activity. Because of the manic ups and the depressive downs, the term bipolar disorder originated and there is no cure for the mental disorder. Whereas, there is not a single risk factor for this condition, some of the possible ones include (1) genetics (it runs in the family) and (2) environment (stressful events or major life changes).

Symptoms that may occur during a manic episode are rapid speech, lack of concentration, high sex drive, decreased need for sleep yet increased energy, increase in impulsivity, and drug or alcohol abuse. The DSM definition for mania is "a distinct period of abnormally and persistently elevated, expansive, or irritable mood". Diagnostic criteria states at least three of the following must be present: high self-esteem, little need for sleep, increased rate of speech, flight of ideas, easily distracted, an increased interest in goals, psychomotor agitation, and increased pursuit of activities with a high risk of danger (DSM-V, 2013).

Symptoms that can occur during the depressive episodes are loss of energy, feeling hopeless, trouble concentrating, irritability, trouble sleeping or sleeping too much, appetite changes, thoughts of death or suicide, and attempting suicide.

The diagnostic criteria for a major depressive episode is that at least four of the following symptoms be present: changes in appetite or weight, sleep or psychomotor activity, decreased energy, feelings of worthlessness or guilt, trouble thinking, concentrating, or making decisions, and thoughts of death or suicidal plans or attempts. Bipolar I disorder involves one or more manic episodes with at least one depressive episode. Bipolar II disorder entails one or more severe depressive episodes with at least one manic episode. Cylothymia is low level depression along with periods of mania. Lastly, Rapid-cycling bipolar disorder occurs when there are at least four episodes of depression and mania. This type affects more women than men (DSM-V, 2013).

Obsessive compulsive disorder (OCD) may be looked upon differently from major depression, schizophrenia, and bipolar disorder. This is because all three have to do with a chemical imbalance in the brain but OCD is more behavioral than anything. OCD is characterized by the presence of obsessions or compulsions or both. It is the fourth most common mental disorder after depression, alcohol/substance abuse, and social phobia. Most people are able to hide this disorder from their family. However, it can cause problems in relationships and interfere with the ability to study or work. If OCD develops in childhood or adolescence, they may avoid socializing with peers or become unable to live independently. The World Health Organization ranks OCD as one of the 10 most handicapping conditions when it comes to lost of income and decreased quality of life (Veale & Roberts, 2014).

The diagnostic criteria for a diagnosis of obsessive compulsive disorder is as follows: (1) either obsession or compulsions (or both) present on most days, (2) obsessions (intrusive thoughts, images, or doubts), which are repetitive, persistent, unwanted, and unpleasant and cause marked concern in most people, (3) compulsions are repetitive behaviors or mental acts that the person feels driven to perform, (4) there are usually attempts to resist a compulsion (although resistance may be minimal in some cases), and (5) carrying out a compulsive act is not essentially pleasurable, but there may be some relief from distress (Veale & Roberts, 2014).

In summary, mental illness in America is more prevalent than most realize. With one out of every five Americans having some type of mental health diagnosis, it is necessary that the appropriate facilities and treatment are made available to those affected. Today, there are still some psychiatric hospitals like the Mayo Clinic and John Hopkins Hospital. Still, most patients choose to utilize outpatient treatment where they can receive psychotherapy and medication prescribed by a psychiatrist. Some outpatient facilities have psychologists available to complete psychological testing for diagnoses purposes (Newsweek, 2014).

CHAPTER 2

The Two That Shall Not Be Ignored

Depression is treatable

The American Psychiatric Association (2017) defines depression as a common but serious medical illness that affects how a person feels, thinks, and acts. There is often feelings of sadness and loss of interest in doing things that you once enjoyed doing. Depression has been known to cause a variety of emotional and physical problems that can hinder a person's ability to function in their homes as well as on their jobs. Some emotional problems that may be seen are crying and isolation. The physical problems can be headaches and extreme tiredness or fatigue. It is important that people who deal with depression know the symptoms and learn how to specialize in self-care and coping.

Fortunately, depression is a treatable condition. There are several anti-depressant medications that can be used to control the symptoms associated with depression. The safer ones with less side effects belong to a group of anti-depressants called Selective Serotonin Reuptake Inhibitors (SSRIs). Some of the most effective SSRIs are Paxil, Lexapro, and Zoloft. In addition to medication, most psychiatrists or psychologists incorporate some form of psychotherapy to enhance the effectiveness of treatment (Feist & Rosenberg, 2014). The psychotherapy could consist of individual sessions, group counseling, and family counseling as needed. Psychotherapy allows the individual to talk about the stressors and/or traumatic events that may have occurred and led to the depressive episodes. During these sessions, coping mechanisms along with therapeutic support are offered to the patient. Combined with the medication, the two are usually successful in treating patients. Group counseling is there to help the individual to see that he or she is not alone. There are others dealing with depression and they learn to be a support to one another. Family counseling is always necessary to ensure that stability is maintained in the home. Depression like all the other mental illnesses not only impacts the individual but impacts the family as a unit. The more support received, the better the prognosis (Feist & Rosenberg, 2014).

Depression in the church

Today, we find very little research on African Americans' mental health. There is even less on African Americans' mental health in congregations. Instead, congregants rely heavily on their religious/spiritual beliefs and practices to cope with mental health issues. The most common one is depression. However, there is not much literature on incorporating religion/spirituality into psychotherapy especially with African American women who are diagnosed more often with depression than African American men (Mengesha & Ward, 2012). Even though, some research shows that faith-based health promotion interventions reduce racial disparities in health screenings for numerous medical conditions; there has not been any health screenings done to show that depression in faith-based settings has even been investigated. Therefore, there remains a need to screen for depression with the Patient Health Questionnaire or PHQ-9 (phqscreeners.com) in African American churches. If done, researchers believe it will show that the prevalence of depression is high, especially among black men. The conclusion reached will be that churches may be an important setting in which to identify depressive symptoms in this already underserved population (Hankerson, Lee, Brawley, Braswell, Wickramaratne, & Weissman, 2015). African Americans compared to White Americans do not utilize mental health services to their fullest. The Centers for Disease Control and Prevention (2017) states, in any two-week period more than 1 in 20 Americans experience depression. Rates are higher among blacks than whites, and yet a report by the surgeon general found that the percentage of blacks who actually get mental health care is only half that of whites. The black church has become the place for emotional triage.

One definition of a triage is the sorting of patients (as in an emergency room) according to the urgency of their need for care (Merriam Webster Dictionary, 2017). This means the black church is comprised of people who may have spiritual, emotional, and/or physical problems and the leader has organized them or prioritized them according to the urgency of their need. A good example that comes to mind has to do with the grieving widow versus the unemployed single mother. It is likely that the grieving widow will be cared for first because that is what the church is accustomed to doing. There are scriptures pertaining to taking care of the widows. It is written in 1 Timothy 5:3-4 (Message Translation) "Take care of any widow who has no one else to care for her. But if she has children or grandchildren, their first responsibility is to show godliness at home and repay their parents by taking care of them. This is something that pleases God." For the church, it does not matter that the widow has someone to take care of her of that her husband may have left her financially wealthy; all that matters is that she is grieving the loss of a loved one. For some reason, in the church, we have limited loss to only death.

Still speaking of widows in 1 Timothy 5:11 (Message Translation) it reads "the younger widows should not be on the list, because their physical desires will overpower their devotion to Christ and they will want to remarry." This scripture is referencing the church supporting the widow. It seems as though there may be difficulty seeing the unemployed single mother as experiencing a loss or losses. For one, she does not have a means to provide for her child or children unless she is receiving government assistance, child support, or help from family and and friends. In addition, it is a loss that she is a single mother. Therefore, she is raising her child or children in the home without a father. The father may or may not be involved but there is nothing like having two parents in the home to nurture a child's growth. This unemployed single mother needs just as much care if not more care from the church as the grieving widow. She needs love, encouragement, and continuous support around her to ensure her emotional, spiritual, and physical stability.

    Finally, concerning depression in African American congregations, it is detrimental to ignore it. Media lets us know on a regular basis that many of the social problems that Americans face are right there in church. The divorce rate in the church is still higher than it should be, sexual abuse of children occurs in the church, sexual exploitation of adults occurs in the church, domestic violence occurs in the church, emotional/verbal abuse occurs in the church and the silent one, financial exploitation of members occurs in the church (Newlife, 2017). All of these social problems can be linked to the mental health or well-being of others. For example, a person may be allowing someone in church leadership to sexually exploit him or her because they went to this trusted person for counseling for depression and received comfort in a way they were not expecting to receive it. The silent one, financial exploitation can occur when members are coerced into giving beyond their tithe and offerings to provide luxuries or non-essentials for church leadership. Some of these people may not have it to give but do so out of feeling obligated or guilty if they do not do it. This happens quite often especially in African American churches (Perkins, 2013).

The Pew Research Center (2009) shows approximately 87% of African Americans as being affiliated with one religious group or another. Nearly 84% of African American women say their religion is very important to them. Over half (59%) of these women attend a religious service on at least a weekly basis. Because the rate of mental illness is so prevalent among the African American population, we know that many of these individuals are in the church. They may be congregants and some of them may be in leadership. Either way, the issue must be addressed and effective interventions must be put in place. These statistics assist us in seeing the need for African American church leaders to be properly trained or educated to address mental health issues in their congregations.

When anxiety is abnormal

Medical News Today (2017) describes anxiety as a generic term for a group of disorders that cause apprehension, nervousness, fear, and worrying. Like depression, anxiety impacts how we feel and behave. It is usually categorized as being mild or severe. Mild anxiety symptoms are vague and unsettling whereas, severe anxiety symptoms can be debilitating and have a serious impact on a person's daily functioning. The causes for anxiety can be environmental, medical, genetic, brain chemistry, or related to a substance abuse issue. Still, anxiety is most commonly triggered by the stress in our lives and outside forces that contribute to the stress. Some external causes of anxiety are stress at work, stress at school, trauma experienced from abuse, and stress about money and finances. Medical causes of anxiety include stress from a serious illness like cancer or stress from the side effects of taking certain medications. Genetic causes of anxiety simply suggest that if a family member suffers from any type of anxiety disorder, it increases the probability that another family member will be diagnosed with the same anxiety disorder. Finally, when it comes to brain chemistry and the causes of anxiety, we need to understand that some individuals have higher levels of neurotransmitters than others and this influences their level of anxiety (Medical News Today, 2017).

It is not uncommon for people to experience a general state of worry or fear (Levine & Munsch, 2014). It normally happens when we are confronted with a challenge that is outside of our normal. Students may experience anxiety right before taking a mid-term or final exam. They understand they have a lot riding on the results so they may worry or fear the outcome. This is a mild form of anxiety. These feelings are easily justified and considered normal. Still it should be noted, that sometimes, we can make ourselves anxious with what is known as "negative self-talk". Anxiety is only considered a problem when symptoms interfere with a person's ability to sleep or a person's daily functioning. Severe anxiety occurs when a reaction is out of proportion with what might be normally expected in a situation (Medical News Today, 2017). A good example of this type of anxiety is every time a person enters a public place, the person fears something bad happening like a shootout occurring.

Types of anxiety and how to recognize them

There are several types of anxiety disorders. The most common types are generalized anxiety disorder (GAD), panic disorder, phobias, social anxiety disorder, obsessive compulsive disorder (OCD), and post-traumatic stress disorder (PTSD). Each disorder takes on their own diagnostic criteria (Feist & Rosenberg, 2014). The diagnostic criteria for OCD is mentioned under the section titled "Depression in African-American Congregations". The diagnostic criteria for GAD is very similar to the criteria for the others mentioned. For a person to be diagnosed with GAD, the following three criteria should be met: (1) excessive worry and anxiety about several different events or activities for at least six months, (2) difficulty controlling the worrying, and (3) having at least three of the following six symptoms associated with anxiety that last six months: restlessness, fatigue, irritability, muscle tension, difficulty sleeping, and difficulty concentrating (DSM-V, 2013). In the church, we may see each of these anxiety disorders manifests in their own way. A panic disorder is defined as a type of anxiety characterized by sudden moments of intense fear (Levine & Munsch, 2014). When a panic attack occurs, a person may start to shake, become confused, dizzy, nauseated and may have difficulty breathing. They normally last about ten minutes but some have lasted for hours. Panic attacks result from frightening experiences like watching someone die or prolonged stress like grieving over a loved one. However, they can be spontaneous and just come out of nowhere.

Social Anxiety Disorder is a phobia characterized by a fear of being judged by people or a fear of being embarrassed in public (Markway & Markway, 2015). Some instances where we see social anxiety appear in others is when a stage performance turns into stage fright, when a failed engagement turns into fear of humiliation, or a failed relationship turns into a fear of being intimate with someone. This disorder can cause people to isolate themselves from being in public situations and avoid human contact to the point that an ordinary life is almost unattainable.

Finally, post-traumatic stress disorder (PTSD) is probably the most overlooked anxiety disorder in the church.

The symptoms include re-experiencing trauma through distressing recollections of events, flashbacks, and nightmares; emotional numbness and avoidance of places, people, and activities that serve as a reminder of the experienced trauma; and an increased arousal such as difficulty sleeping and concentrating, feeling jumpy, and being easily irritated and angered. PTSD is diagnosed after a person experiences symptoms for at least one month following a traumatic event. However, symptoms may not appear until several months or even years later (Anxiety and Depression Association of America (ADAA, 2017). Diagnostic criteria for PTSD applies to adults, adolescents, and children six years of age and older. For a person to receive the diagnosis, he or she must have been exposed to an actual or threatened death, serious injury, or sexual violation. In addition, one of the following must be present: (1) spontaneous, involuntary, and intrusive memories of the traumatic event, (2) recurrent frightening dreams, (3) flashbacks or dissociative reactions to traumatic events, and (4) prolonged psychological distress when exposed to symbolization or reminders of the traumatic events (ADAA, 2017).

Three percent of Americans experience anxiety disorders. It may seem common and expected for most individuals. For those dealing with it on a regular basis, it can be frightening and debilitating (Turner, 2017). Those who have regular panic attacks live in constant fear because they do not know when or where one may occur. It can easily impair their daily functioning whereas it may keep them from going to school or showing up at work on a daily basis. They sometimes isolate themselves just like those who are struggling with social anxiety disorder. A social anxiety diagnosis can prevent a person from attending or feeling comfortable in the church. They are constantly fearing whether people are going to judge them or whether they will do something to cause embarrassment. Many in the church are suffering from PTSD. Some go to church to try and escape the repetitive reminders of the traumatic event. Others have PTSD that resulted from a traumatic experience in the church. Either way, trauma can cause stress. If it is not treated, it can leave lasting scars on the individual and their families. People with anxiety disorders will need some form of treatment to help them feel like they are a normal part of society. Therefore, professional and/or Christian counseling can be instrumental when it comes to addressing mental health issues in the African-American congregation (Turner, 2017).

CHAPTER 3

Mental Illness
Why Is The Church Silent?

Fictional Scenarios Depicting Mental Illness In The Church

There is a made for television movie titled "The Undershepherd" (Parr, Eubanks, Tomosunas, & Aronson, 2012) which highlights some of the dysfunction which still exists in today's African-American church. Although, this is certainly not true, the first impression most people will have is that this is your typical black or African-American church. Still, we can use this movie to understand that we may find some dysfunction from each scene represented throughout the African-American church. It is almost impossible for any church to stand with a whole lot of confusion because eventually the dysfunction will lead to an unfavorable end. Because some churches may have less confusion than others, they are still able to stand and practice their beliefs.

"The Undershepherd" (Parr, Eubanks, Tomosunas, & Aronson, 2012) stars a very well-known cast to include such great African-American actors like Bill Cobbs, Lou Gossett, Jr., Isaiah Washington, Keith David, Malinda Williams, Elise Neal, Clifton Powell and Lamaan Rucker to name a few. The movie is centered upon corruption, greed, and power in the black church. The longtime Bishop was suddenly hit with one major change that many church leaders are facing in today's church. That change is contemporary (occurring in the present). Meaning, in today's church there has been a significant shift from traditional to contemporary worship services. He learned that traditional (long established) is being replaced by contemporary. In other words, what worked well for so many years no longer works now. To assist with the change, Bishop decided to allow his Senior Pastor to spend more time in the pulpit ministering to the congregation. This did not work for them. They wanted and needed more than the traditional preachers could offer.

The congregation was plagued with deep spiritual/mental issues identified as adultery, mental illness, eating disorders, and abortion subsequently. The people wanted someone who was not afraid to address these current issues or contemporary social problems. They wanted someone who would make them feel good about what was going on with them. For them, the preacher for the job was one of the young ministers on staff. Eventually, the Bishop and the Pastor were replaced by this minister as the Senior Pastor. The congregation was so enlightened by his preaching style and prophetic teachings, they overlooked his power and control issues. This young minister became obsessed with living a luxurious lifestyle. He bought fancy cars, diamond rings, and expensive clothing (Parr, Eubanks, Tomosunas, & Aronson, 2012).

Under his leadership, the church began to prosper financially and the media was monitoring their success through live television filming. There were some who had been in leadership for many years at the church who were not impressed with anything the young preacher did and saw that the church was headed towards destruction. The first spiritual issue we saw was "the sin of adultery". The undershepherd started having sexual affairs with single and married women in the church. One of the affairs led to him impregnating the deacon's daughter and he convinced his assistant to take the young lady to have an abortion. There were complications and the young lady ended up in the hospital fighting for her life

(Parr, Eubanks, Tomosunas, & Aronson, 2012).

In the meantime, the undershepherd's wife exhibited symptoms related to depression, stress, and anxiety. He was verbally and emotionally abusive to her and complained of her weight because he knew she had the eating disorder called bulimia nervosa. Not only was she suffering from bulimia but she was also dealing with infertility. She was unable to give the undershepherd a child. His wife became so disoriented that she was hiding the disorder by spending time down in their home's basement where she kept exercise equipment and the vomit in plastic bags from her disorder (Parr, Eubanks, Tomosunas, & Aronson, 2012). There was a female member in the congregation who had a mental illness and was taking medication. The undershepherd convinced her that she did not need the medicine. He convinced her before the congregation that the mental illness was demonic and that after he prayed for her, she would be healed. As the lies and deceit were revealed, this female member returned to the church with a gun. Her psychotic symptoms escalated from not taking her medications and she was escorted from the church by the police hopefully to a psychiatric hospital (Parr, Eubanks, Tomosunas, & Aronson, 2012).

First, it appears that the Bishop and other church leaders had no idea about the mental health issues going on within the congregation. They had a minister on staff whose wife was clearly depressed, filled with anxiety, obsessed with eating, and sick with an eating disorder. Second, the Bishop and other church leaders did not see that their young minister was struggling with some mental health issues of his own. It was clear that he was suffering from delusions of grandeur (a false sense of one's own importance). At one point in the movie, the undershepherd referred to himself as being "God". Lastly, the undershepherd was not properly trained to address mental health issues in the congregation. As a result, his lack of training contributed to a psychological/emotional breakdown of a church member. The female member believed her leader and therefore, did not follow the orders of the doctor to take her medications to keep the symptoms of her mental illness under control (Parr, Eubanks, Tomosunas, & Aronson, 2012).

There is an ongoing television series produced by Oprah Winfrey titled "Greenleaf" (Winfrey & Virgo, 2016) which also looks at the continuing dysfunction in the African American church. Winfrey stars in the television series on her network (OWN) along with Keith David, Lynn Whitfield, Lamaan Rucker, and Merle Dandridge. The series is about a megachurch in Memphis, Tennessee that is filled with secrets and lies. The series is named after the family that leads the church. The patriarch of the family is the Bishop and the matriarch is the first lady who also preaches. Their younger daughter named Faith was sexually abused by her maternal uncle for years and the family never acknowledged the abuse. The maternal uncle served as the church's attorney. His hurt started in the Greenleaf home and because he did not get the counseling needed, he has resorted to hurting others (young girls). Faith was so hurt that she became depressed to the point where she committed suicide by drowning herself. The family continues to cover up the truth until their estranged daughter, Grace returns home after being gone for twenty years. Grace is an ordained pastor whom her sister confided in about the abuse. Grace told their parents who refused to believe her. When the parents questioned Faith, she denied it because she did not want to destroy the family nor ruin the reputation of the church. This is another indication there may have been African-American church leaders who were not trained to address mental health issues in the congregation (Winfrey & Virgo, 2016).

There has been no mention of a pastoral counselor or

Christian counselor on staff. Instead, they all seem to be caught up in status, power, money, keeping secrets, telling lies, and keeping themselves out of jail. Faith's mental and emotional well-being were never addressed and it's likely that because they were not, she could not handle the overwhelming stress it caused her so she decided to end her life and pain through committing suicide (Winfrey & Virgo, 2016).

Real life scenarios depicting mental illness in the church

We know that both "The Undershepherd" and "Greenleaf" have aired on television and the characters are factitious but yet they portray real life issues. Nevertheless, there are some real life individuals who are perfect for these scenarios. The first one I will discuss is Candace Gorham who is a former ordained evangelist who is now a licensed professional counselor. Gorham (2013) wrote a book titled: The Ebony Exodus Project: Why some black women are walking out on religion-----and others should too. The book is based on Evangelist Gorham's life in the church while suffering from major depression and suicidal thoughts at the same time.

Gorham (2013) has granted several interviews behind the reason for writing the book. Gorham moved around quite a bit as a child. When it came to attending the church, she was familiar with both Jehovah's Witness and African Methodist Episcopal (AME) churches. At the age of 18, Gorham started attending a non-denominational church in which her sister and her husband founded. Gorham described herself as taking church very seriously and being really into it. She relates that she was not only preaching, but prophesying, laying on hands, casting out demons, and speaking in tongues. Gorham met her husband in college and he joined the church with her and they worked in the ministry together as husband and wife.

Years later, Gorham (2013) states she and her husband fell on some really hard times. They kept wondering what they were doing wrong. They were fasting, praying, and believing that things would get better but they never did. They had a child to feed and eventually, life circumstances began to weigh her down. Gorham states she became very depressed and suicidal. She thought about death all the time. At this time, Gorham and her husband were a part of a small mega church with a little over one thousand members. She went to the first lady because she did not feel her pastor was very personable. Gorham spoke with her about her depression and suicidal thoughts. Gorham recalls the first lady did not have any answers and asked the pastor to join them for their session. Gorham (2013) states he listened but continued to tell her to pray more and to attend church even more than she and her family were already attending.

Gorham (2013) states this is when she received the revelation that religion was not her answer. She remembers crying and becoming more depressed after leaving her appointment with the pastor and first lady. Gorham decided to seek professional mental health counseling on her own telling only her husband and mother. She was diagnosed with clinical depression and was put on medication to alleviate the symptoms. Gorham relates she became consumed with guilt over her condition and felt torn between her beliefs. Even though she was feeling better, she no longer felt comfortable being at the church or any other church knowing their beliefs about mental illness. The church leaders never suggested that she receive outside professional counseling. Gorham understood that her mental health diagnosis was not something that she could just pray away. She needed a physical intervention to help her cope with the illness. Since that time, Gorham (2013) has walked away from the church and her religious beliefs regarding "Jesus is all that you need". She states this is one of the biggest lies told to the church. People must be proactive in seeing about their physical and mental well-being. There are doctors for a reason. In the Bible, Luke was a physician. Counselors or therapists exist for a reason. The Bible reads in Proverbs 11:14 "where there is no counsel, the people fall; but in the multitude of counselors there is safety" (NKJV). This is saying that wise counsel is safe for us. It's better to receive counseling from others than to try and handle things on your own.

According to Christian Today (2013), another case occurred in 2013 in Macon, Georgia when a well-known African-American Baptist church pastor suffering from major depression committed suicide. On a Sunday morning, the pastor sent his wife and children to church ahead of him and after he did not show up to preach the morning's message, his wife returned home looking for him but she was not expecting to find what she found. The pastor was sitting in his truck dead from a self-inflicted gunshot wound. The family and the church family were devastated and at a loss for words. The pastor did not share his condition with his parishioners because he feared they would no longer trust him to be their leader. The pastor's immediate family knew about his diagnosis and that he was in treatment. He was taking medications to treat the depression but the medications brought on some physical challenges. He obviously felt even more depressed after losing his parents and some others who were an integral part of his support system. Obviously, all these circumstances begin to overwhelm this pastor to the point whereas he no longer wanted to live. One of his pastor friends whom he spoke to on a regular basis stated "There are some things you just can't pray away. Some things are more physical than spiritual." Leaders need to be trained to be able to distinguish between the two in order to assist their congregants if needed (Christian Today, 2013).

Before concluding this section, the author must mention that not only would African American church leaders need training to address mental health issues in their congregations, but also church leaders from other racial backgrounds. Best-selling author and megachurch pastor, Rick Warren was very verbal and open with sharing information about his son, Matthew Warren's struggle with borderline personality disorder. After receiving much treatment, his inability to cope led to his untimely death. Matthew committed suicide by shooting himself at the age of 27. A personality disorder is best treated with talk therapy. In some instances, medications can be used to treat it. A person can receive a lifetime of therapy to try and cope with the symptoms. Most persons suffering from mental illness just want to live as normal a life as possible (Christianity Today, 2013).

Mental illness and mass shootings

During the past few years, we have seen an increase in mass shootings not only in the schools but in the church as well. Some have argued there is little connection between mental illness and mass shootings while others believe there is a clear link between the two (Los Angeles Times, 2018). No one can say that mental illness is the primary reason for mass shootings because we all understand that environmental, sociocultural and political factors may play a role. Still, there is evidence stating that mass shootings that took place in the United States from 1900 through 2017, almost 60% of them were committed by people who had been diagnosed as mentally ill or showed signs of having a serious mental disorder prior to the attack (Fox News, 2018). We also must look at the fact that most mass murders end up committing suicide which is a form of mental illness in itself.

Duwe (2018) says "typically what we see with those who carry out a mass public shooting is that they do suffer from a mental disorder, in some cases it's diagnosable, or there's some information from friends and family that indicates they suffered from mental illness". According to Fox News (2018), paranoid schizophrenia is more common among mass murders than any other mental illness. Research by the Los Angeles Times revealed that only one-third of the people who have committed mass shootings in the U.S. since 1900 had sought or received mental health care prior to their attacks. Men are less likely than women to seek mental health treatment and 99% of the mass shootings in the U.S were at the hands of men. This suggests that most shooters did not seek or receive care they may have needed (L.A. Times, 2018).

Like religion and mental illness, there is a stigmatization when it comes to mass shootings and mental illness. Mental Health Professionals do not want society to think that mental health issues are not being controlled in the United States. Therefore, some say it is more a gun control issue than a mental health issue while others believe that both mental health and gun control are equally to blame (L.A. Times, 2018). The New York Times (2018) reports that mental illness may not be the reason for mass shootings but angry young men who harbor violent fantasies. Sometimes, we miss it early on with the signs of oppositional defiant disorder and conduct disorder which are still mental health diagnoses. In these cases, mentoring our young men and instilling strong moral values in them early may assist with eliminating the onset of mental disorders that we see exhibited in these angry young males with violent fantasies.

Personal Testimonies

Living with mental illness is not the way any person would chose to live. People do not choose mental illness; mental illness chooses people. Once that chemical imbalance takes place, no one knows the severity of the impact. Will it stop at depression; will it spiral to bipolar disorder or will it spin out of control to schizophrenia? This can be a terrifying experience for a person to know that without medication, he or she may be unable to control their thoughts and behaviors. One great thing is most can control their actions with proper guidance and direction. This is where mental health professionals can do the most good.

Imagine being on the dean's list at one of the most prestigious universities in the country. You are an aerospace engineer major just waiting to graduate and secure your dream job at NASA. When all of a sudden, the academic pressures start to weigh heavily on you. You begin to stress more and more and now negative thoughts have entered your mind. Before you know it, you are having panic attacks and you become over fearful about everyday situations. Now imagine this fear turning to paranoia and now your thoughts have become delusional. By the time you realize what is going on, the chemical imbalance has been prolonged to the point of paranoia schizophrenia. Now, you feel like your life is over because you have to take psychotropic medications and go to counseling on a weekly basis. The medication side effects prevent you from functioning in the classroom and now your paranoia thoughts lead to you dropping out of college with only a year to go before graduation.

You are a person who has been battling depression since you were a teenager. Now, imagine yourself so immersed in the church that you are reading and studying your Bible. You are preaching to people on Sunday and believing God for a change in your financial situation because you are currently unemployed with bills to pay and no one available to help you. Because you are a faithful tithe payer and sometimes give over and beyond in your offerings, you thought the church would help you financially. Instead, they said they couldn't and you need to figure it out on your own. While you are trying to figure it out, the air condition unit goes out during the hottest month of the year. The money you have been paying towards your rent, you find out the homeowner has been keeping it for personal reasons and now the house is in foreclosure and you don't have any money and nowhere to go. The more you pray, the worst things seem to get. You are now depressed and crying every day. You begin to believe that your situation will never change. You stop believing in the church and you are physically, mentally and emotionally drained. Suicidal thoughts enter your mind because you feel worthless and as if no one loves or cares for you. You start to isolate yourself from others and you are so far down in the dumps, you feel like you have reached the point of no return. Depression is now controlling you and you are no longer controlling the depression.

    You are a strong, outgoing, independent person who enjoys life. You love to travel, shop, and attend events. Now imagine going to a concert to see your favorite artist and gunfire breaks out. You panic and run away from the building trying to find your car. When you get to your car, you are so startled that you have to get someone else to drive you home. You don't sleep at all that night. The next day every time you try to fall to sleep, you hear the gunshots and see yourself running from them. Now, you fear something is going to happen to you or someone close to you. Every time you hear a loud noise, you are reminded of the gunshots that were fired at the concert. Your friend invites you to a party at a community center; you go because you need to get your mind off what happened at the concert. After you enter the building and see all the people, you begin to panic all over again. Now, you are fearful of going into places with a large number of people. The panic attacks are occurring every time you hear of someone shooting. You refuse to go to counseling because you keep telling yourself that you can overcome the fear. You try and pray it a way but will not go to church because you have convinced yourself that too many people will be there. Now, every day, you are living your life closed in with the fear of the unknown. It impacts your ability to work and your ability to even go outside of your home. You are having panic attacks every time you hear a loud noise and you become very anxious whenever too many people are in the same room with you.

Remember, if these things happened to them, it can happen to you.

CHAPTER 4

There Is Safety Because There Is Help

MHP – Train the Trainer

God says in Hosea 4:6 that "my people are destroyed for lack of knowledge" (KJV). The Bible stresses the importance of receiving good teaching to expand your knowledge so you can have a better understanding of how to live life. Jesus trained his disciples for three years before He released them into the world to perform miracles, heal the sick, and cast out demons. He wanted to make sure they were trained or equipped to do the things that He did. From this, it appears that training is needed for us to do what we need to do for each other. An effective training program for church leaders should be simple to follow and easy to implement. Most Pastors/Bishops do not have a whole lot of time so flexibility would be key to them actually participating in the training and receiving what is needed. Therefore, the researcher proposes a certification program titled Church Mental Health Advisor (CMHA). The certification training should be done by a mental health professional (MHP) who has a ministry background to demonstrate understanding from both the mental health and ministry perspectives.

Conditions of Participation

The criteria for participation in training program are: (1) the individual must be a pastor, associate pastor, or designated leader, if there is not a licensed professional counselor (LPC) or therapist on staff and (2) if the pastor, associate pastor, or designated leader does not have a mental health background, they will sign a Memorandum of Understanding (MOU), Appendix A, to refer parishioners to a trusted mental health professional if the parishioner agrees to treatment for depression or any other mental illness. The length of the training program will be three hours a day for three days after which the church leader will receive certification as a Church Mental Health Advisor (CMHA).

How this training program benefits the church

The training program will consist of three major components: (1) The church leaders' role in mental health (2) Understanding the Spiritual versus Mental, and (3) Helping families cope. First, the MHP should educate the trainees on their role when it comes to advising congregants on mental health issues. There is a form titled the PHQ-9, Appendix B, which is a health questionnaire that contains questions that can be used by the CMHA to screen for depression. Church leaders or designated leaders can be trained on how to use this form to screen for depression.

If the scoring indicates depression, the certified CMHA should proceed by speaking with the parishioner regarding obtaining professional help and encourage follow-up. The choice should be made by the parishioner and/or their family as to whether they desire assistance from a professional outside of the church. If requested, the certified CMHA can assist with locating resources and making referrals on the parishioner's behalf. As a support, it is acceptable if the parishioner wants the CMHA to go with them for their initial mental health appointment.

The second component should be taught for clarity on the difference between spiritual and mental issues. Research indicates having a better understanding of the difference can be key in addressing mental health issues in the church (Stetzer, 2013). Historically, mental illness was considered a spiritual condition. Those suffering from mental illness were told to pray more like Candace Gorham (2013) or that there was a demonic spirit within that needed to be cast out. Unfortunately, today, some church leaders still believe this to be true even though research has proven differently. As the movement shifted towards people seeing mental illness as a physical condition, the church became silent and refused to address the issue leaving those impacted with no other choice but to seek help from a professional or ignore the problem to see if it would go away.

Understanding the spiritual versus the mental should focus on explaining causes of mental illness, the types of mental illness, signs and symptoms (diagnostic criteria) and treatments used for mental illness (Stetzer, 2013). Crisis situations should be addressed so CMHAs can learn about de-escalation and who to call for help when needed to protect themselves and their congregants if the person becomes irate or violent. Scenarios or case examples can be used to help church leaders identify when the matter has gone beyond a spiritual realm to a physical realm. For example, depression can be identified as a spiritual or physical condition. Spiritually, a person may be sad or feel hopeless about their life and the direction it has turned. A pastor or designated leader may talk with the person and discover they experienced the recent loss of a friend and has difficulty accepting it. After a few (3 to 4) counseling sessions, the person has reported decreased sadness and feelings of hopelessness. The person reports feeling more accepting of the friend's death which indicates more spiritual versus physical. If the person continues to report sadness and hopelessness with no change after receiving counseling, there may be a need for medication which immediately shifts it to the physical realm. Anytime medication is needed, it means something is out of alignment with the body and the medicine is needed to bring alignment back.

Helping families cope is the third component of this training program followed by certification. The third component becomes probably the most important one of them all. CMHAs should advise not only the diagnosed parishioner about mental illness and the options available to them for treatment but their family as well. They should encourage parishioner and the family to keep all professional therapy appointments and assist with transportation if needed. Congregants should be encouraged to take their medications as instructed by the physician and family members should take an active role in educating themselves regarding mental illness (American Psychological Association, 2017). The CMHAs may form support groups and develop recreational activities for the mentally ill and their families. The goal is to let families know the church understands and they are not alone in the struggle.

CMHA Certification Training Program

Based upon the research literature, these three components have been successful in treating those suffering from any type of mental illness. When support systems are in place, mentally ill patients tend to be more proactive in seeking treatment, staying in treatment, and with taking medications (Morrison-Valfre, 2017). A church training program on depression may look like this: (1) Church leaders (Pastor, Associate Pastor, or Designated Leader) will be chosen to attend CMHA certification training to become equipped to advise on mental health issues like depression that may arise within their congregation. The first session will aid the trainee in understanding why it is important for church leaders to know about mental health issues, including depression. Their role will be clearly defined in terms of their responsibilities to the other church leaders, their congregants, and their community. As the church mental health advisor, the trainee needs to form a mental health committee within the church. The committee can consist of church leaders from different auxiliaries within the church for consulting purposes only. The mental health committee will be the governing body for the church mental health advisor. This will protect the CMHA with decision making, protecting confidentiality, and adherence to the ethics and laws that protect the mentally ill. In the event, the trainee is unsure of how to handle a situation, there is a team in place to offer support.

The trainee must agree to keep all information shared by the congregants as confidential. The only exception is when consulting needs to be done with the mental health committee or when there is a threat to harm themselves or others. The trainee will make sure both the parishioner and their family understand this information prior to them signing the agreement for church mental health advising. Also, the trainee has a responsibility to protect the community from mentally ill persons who have the potential to become violent or dangerous. In such an event, the proper authorities should be notified. In most cases, this would be the police who will contact a psychiatric hospital or other mental health professionals. The MHP will talk about current mental health statistics and recent church events related to mental health issues. A good example would be the 2015 massacre shooting that occurred at an AME church in Charleston, South Carolina (Smith & Hawes, 2017). Even though the shooter requested that his mental health information not be revealed, it was mentioned in the article that the shooter suffered from mental illnesses such as social anxiety disorder and schizoid personality disorder.

During the second session, statistics and factual information on depression will be supplied to trainee in the form of handouts. The MHP will teach this information from a Power Point Presentation if the church has the capability. If not, the MHP will use handouts for teaching purposes. These handouts will define depression and other depressive disorders commonly found in the church. The trainee will be educated on the signs and symptoms of depression along with the different types of medication used to treat depression. (2) The spiritual versus the mental component will be addressed by the MHP in terms of providing definitions and a concrete understanding of how to separate the two terms. Mental is defined as relating to the mind or an intellectual process while spiritual is pertaining to the spirit or the soul (Wikidiff, 2017). This lets us know we are dealing with two different entities, the mind and the spirit. Therefore, separation is necessary to address them appropriately. In reality, we just cannot pray or read scripture enough for some things to go away. This is because in some cases, the issues are physical, chemical, or physiological. Prayer can help but more prayer is not the only remedy for mental illness. Medicine may be required as well.

Stetzer (2013) wrote an article discussing his beliefs about the spiritual and mental when it comes to the church. He states "part of our belief system is that God changes everything, and that because Christ lives in us, everything in our hearts and minds should be fixed. But that doesn't mean we don't sometimes need medical help and community help to do those things." Stetzer (2013) was praying with one of his members and reading scriptures with him as often as possible. Still, this member continued to take his medication. When he was taking his medications, he seemed be at his healthiest and was whole. This helped Stetzer to realize as a pastor that the key word in mental illness is "illness". This member was sick and not just struggling spiritually, but actually struggling physically and there is a major difference.

There is nothing wrong with seeking medical help for our mental health just like we do for our physical health. Also, there is nothing wrong with the community coming together to support the mentally ill just like the community comes together to support those with cancer. There is nothing wrong with taking medications for our mental health conditions just like we take medications for our physical conditions. Our experiences are not the same as others' experiences. Just because biblical counseling alone worked for an individual does not mean it will work for everyone else. Biblical counseling is good for spiritual or personal struggles but they are not the same as mental illness (Stetzer, 2013).

The MHP will use scriptures from the Bible concerning physicians. Luke was known as the beloved physician (Colossians 4:14, KJV). There are other instances of physicians mentioned in Genesis 50:2, KJV where they were asked to embalm Jacob's body. In 2 Chronicles 16:2, KJV, Asa consults physicians for his foot ailment and it is even mentioned in Mark 5:26, KJV that the woman with an issue of blood spent her money going to physicians before coming to Jesus for her healing (La Vista Church of Christ, 2016). These examples will assist the trainee with understanding that physicians have always existed and there is nothing wrong with going to one for medical help. We can seek medical help and still have faith in God at the same time.

Tim Keller (2010) wrote a profound statement within his article about the four models of counseling in pastoral ministry. He writes: "We must be aware of giving people the impression that through individual repentance for sin they should be able to undo their personal problems. While we cannot fall into believing all problems are chemically based and require medication, we cannot believe that all problems are simply a matter of lacking spiritual disciplines. Schizophrenia, bipolar depression, and other psychological problems are rooted in physiological problems that call for more than talk therapy, but they call for medical treatment."

The MHP can use scenarios to include crisis situations brought on by depression that may occur in the church as interactive exercises between the MHP and the trainee. The trainee will have the opportunity to role play how he or she would react if a mental health crisis should arise in the church. For example, a person with paranoia schizophrenia may accuse an usher of taking their money even after he or she willingly placed the money into the offering plate. The person may become very loud and start to yell at the usher. The mental health advisor could use de-escalation in this situation.

To do this, the appropriate thing is to not take sides but ask the person if he or she could step out of the worship service with you and the usher to resolve the situation. If there is another family member present, it is important to invite this person so the parishioner will not feel as if you are trying to take advantage of the situation. If the person agrees to walk out with you, never turn your back, allow the person to walk in front of you. Do not argue but inquire of the parishioner about how you can make the situation right. If the person refuses to walk out and continues to be loud, this is when security should be called or when other committee members will have to assist with the escorting. If none of these things work, police authorities should be notified. Real life scenarios are good and effective training tools (MindTools, 2017).

Next, the MHP will introduce the PHQ-9 depression screening form to the trainees. The MHP will explain the purpose of the form, go over the questions on the form, and train on how to score the form. The trainee will be given the scoring chart to go along with the form to show the parishioner's level of depression. At the end of the session, the MHP will discuss available resources and provide a list of possible resources available in the community to the trainee. The MHP will encourage the trainee to research other available community resources not listed and collaborate with resources to let them know about the mental health training program within their church.

(3) During the last component which is helping families cope with the individual diagnosed with depression, the trainee will understand his or her role as an advocate and spiritual support to the parishioner and their family. The trainee will learn that if a family is referred to a mental health professional, their role as church mental health advisor has really just begun. This congregant and their family will rely on the CMHA for moral, emotional, and spiritual support. They may utilize the CMHA for transportation to and from appointments until they are comfortable enough with the MHP to go on their own. The trainee will learn how to develop a trusting relationship with the parishioner and the family so they will be comfortable sharing family history and other private information regarding the mental health condition.

The trainee should work with the parishioner and family to develop a trusting relationship with their MHP. This can be demonstrated by encouraging them to ask the MHP questions about the condition and prescribed medications. If there are any concerns or things they do not understand in reference to side effects or what they can and cannot do, they should inquire of the MHP. These things assist with building rapport. If the parishioner does not want their family to know about their mental health issues, the trainee should respect this and may have to develop a support system within the church such as a support group meeting at least once a month with others facing some mental challenges. This could be a possible collaboration between community churches (National Alliance on Mental Illness, 2017).

The trainee can set up an appointment calendar to keep track of all the advisees' mental health appointments, support group times, birthdays, and special occasions for them. It is always good to participate in celebrating their accomplishments and encouraging them during their failures. The trainee will learn how to assist the parishioner and family with keeping a calendar of appointments as well as a pill scheduler to alleviate missed medication dosages. To ensure they feel included and as normal as possible, they should always be invited to attend church activities and even have recreational activities for them during their support group meeting times. Part of the reason why it is difficult to acknowledge mental illness in the church is because there is still a perception that Christians are not suppose to have these issues. If we are not ashamed of someone getting a virus, we should not be ashamed of someone having a chemical imbalance that leads the person to a lifelong struggle with depression (Stetzer, 2013). If church leaders' can participate in this training, it may be that the church itself will have a better understanding of mental illness and will be more compassionate and willing to provide a nurturing environment for them to worship and enhance their spiritual beliefs (Mental Health Grace Alliance, 2014). The primary purpose of the training program is to ensure that the church will no longer remain silent about mental illness but speak out and advocate for those in need of the services.

Now that you know this help is available to you, what is your next move? You can start by answering the seven questions to follow.

THOUGHT PROVOKING QUESTIONS

1. After reading this book, what does mental illness mean to you?

_____
_____
_____
_____
_____
_____
_____
_____
_____
_____
_____

2. Prior to reading this book, what kind of training had you received regarding mental illness/mental health?

_____
_____
_____
_____
_____
_____
_____
_____
_____
_____
_____
_____
_____

3. Explain your experience with mental illness in the church by providing examples.

_____
_____
_____
_____
_____
_____
_____
_____
_____
_____

4. Are you aware of community resources available to the mentally ill and what services they provide? If so, what are they?

_____
_____
_____
_____
_____
_____
_____

5. What do you believe about church pastors receiving or not receiving mental health training?

_____
_____
_____
_____

6. If you are a pastor or community leader, are you willing to support the mentally ill and their families within your congregation?

7. After reading this book, what do you think about participating in a church training program on mental health?

NO MORE SILENCE

There Is Safety
JOURNAL

Whenever you release something that has been plaguing you, then the healing process can begin. It is never good to hold the hurt and pain inside. Here is a journal for you to finally release those things that have been negatively affecting you.

~JOURNAL~

~JOURNAL~

~JOURNAL~

~JOURNAL~

~JOURNAL~

~JOURNAL~

~JOURNAL~

~JOURNAL~

~JOURNAL~

~JOURNAL~

~JOURNAL~

~JOURNAL~

~JOURNAL~

~JOURNAL~

~JOURNAL~

~JOURNAL~

~JOURNAL~

~JOURNAL~

~JOURNAL~

~JOURNAL~

~JOURNAL~

~JOURNAL~

~JOURNAL~

~JOURNAL~

~JOURNAL~

ABOUT THE AUTHOR

Being very grateful for my upbringing, I am privileged to say that I was born and raised in Wilcox County, Alabama in a small city called Camden. I was reared the first 10 years of my life in a four-room house with seven other family members in a small town known as Possum Bend. We had a front room (living room), back room (spare bedroom), kitchen and bedroom. There was no inside bathroom or outhouse. We had what was known as a slop-jar (portable potty). My mother washed clothes in cold water with a washing board and rinsed them in hot water before hanging them on the clothesline to dry.

I experienced working in the fields, but it was not picking cotton. We picked tomatoes, cucumbers, corn, watermelon, field peas, okra, etc. We grew up around berry patches and plum trees. We had a pump that supplied our water and even though our living was substandard, we were happy as a family.

Over the years, I watched God bless us to move into a four-bedroom, two-bathroom apartment with upstairs only to lose it to water damage from a fire and we had to move into a small mobile home that barely had indoor plumbing again. This story was shared to help you understand the ups and downs, we sometimes experience in life. As the changes take us up and down, our mood goes along with it and it bounces between happiness and sadness. This is the way mental illness works.

Thankfully, amid the ups and the downs, I have seen God do some amazing things in my life! Being a child raised by a single parent on welfare benefits with six other siblings in the household, the odds were against us and statistics said I would not achieve my current educational status in life. However, I have always been one determined to succeed despite obstacles. Both my parents managed to finish high school and most of my siblings did the same. Still, I wanted and needed more.

My mother was and will forever be the greatest woman I know. I watched her struggle with trying to provide for her family on a daily basis with what she had. She knew how to make ends meet. Because of this, I promised myself that I would do all I could to make her struggle a little easier. This led to me graduating high school, completing my undergraduate education and finishing a Masters in Counseling Psychology and a Masters in Social Work. Recently, I graduated with a Doctor of Ministry degree.

My education helped me to secure employment that allowed me to help my family. Not only was I able to assist them financially but it motivated them to establish themselves financially as well. Iron really does sharpen iron. Even though, I don't have a job with a six-figure salary or even close to it, I am blessed to help others with what I do have.

Answering my call to ministry in 2010 has truly been life changing. I have experienced disappointments, church hurt, setbacks, broken relationships/friendships and loss loved ones. On the other end, I have experienced spiritual growth, established a personal relationship with Jesus Christ, developed my leadership abilities, learned how to worship and walk into my purpose and destiny.

Personally, I have handled depression since I was 19 years old. It was so bad that I almost had a nervous breakdown from academic pressures and fear of failure; but, with the help of a praying mother, we did pray my way through without outpatient mental health treatment or medication. However, when I came out of the world and entered the church, the depression returned. The root of it stemmed from harassment, betrayal, control and manipulation in my place of employment for 13 years. I connected with the Employee Assistance Program and sought individual counseling only to find myself counseling my counselor. We both agreed that I was fine.

Next, there would be church hurt after church hurt primarily from those in the Pulpit. This time I sought Christian Counseling only to be told after my initial session again, that I seem fine and I could come back if I felt the need for additional sessions. Because of the pain, in my world, church leadership could not be trusted and now I couldn't get wise counsel from the professionals either. I have friends who are licensed therapists, counselors and social workers who thought I was joking whenever I tried to discuss my need for counseling.
Therefore, I felt pressed to speak out and say something. After praying to God about it, He told me to use my education, training, the Word, and life experiences to pull myself through. He told me to exercise, get massages, socialize, and enjoy life as much as possible. He told me to use ministry as my therapy and when I am home alone, to use my telephone as my therapy.

Now, my family and friends will understand why I call and text them so often. My struggle helped me to truly understand that many don't have this advantage and therefore, I wrote this book and designed this training program with them in mind. Proverbs 11:14 says "Where no counsel is, the people fall: but in the multitude of counselors there is safety" (KJV). The message version tells us "without good direction, people lose their way: the more wise counsel you follow, the better your chances."

If you are interested in this CMHA training program, please contact me by email (iprae@yahoo.com), phone, (334) 568-9995 or mail, P O Box 2314104, Montgomery, AL 36123.

BIBLIOGRAPHY

American Psychiatric Association. (2017). DSM History. Retrieved from https://www.psychiatry.org

American Psychological Association. (2017). How to cope when a loved one has a serious mental illness. Retrieved from http://www.apa.org

Anxiety and Depression Association of America. (2017). Symptoms of PTSD. Retrieved from www.adaa.org

Brown, V. & Keith, D. (2013). African American women & mental well-being: The triangulation of race, gender, and socioeconomic status. Cambridge University Press.

Christian Today. (2013). Pastor Teddy Parker commits suicide as congregation waits for him after confessing sometimes he "can't feel God". Retrieved from www.christiantoday.com

Christianity Today. (2013). Rick Warren tells story of son's suicide on CNN. Retrieved from www.christianitytoday.com

Cockerham, W. C. (2016). Sociology of mental disorder. Birmingham, Alabama: Rutledge.

Cohen, D. & Crabtree, B. (2006). Qualitative Research Guidelines Project. Retrieved from http://www.qualres.org/HomeLinc-3684.htm

Creswell, J. W. (2007). Qualitative inquiry & research design: Choosing among five approaches (2nd ed). Thousand Oaks, CA: Sage.

Creswell, J. W. (2009). Research design: Qualitative, quantitative, and mixed methods approaches (3rd ed.) Thousand Oaks, CA: Sage.

Creswell, J. W. (2014). Research design: Qualitative, quantitative, and mixed methods approaches. Thousand Oaks, California: Sage.

Dempsey, K., Butler, S. K., & Gaither, L. (2015). Black churches and mental health professionals: Can this collaboration work? Journal of Black Studies, Vol. 47(1); pp. 73-87. DOI: 10.1177/0021934715613588 jbs.sagepub.com

Deutsch, A. (2013). The mentally ill in America: A history of their care and treatment from colonial times. New York, New York: Columbia University Press.

Falk, G. (2001). Stigma: How we treat outsiders. Amherst, New York: Prometheus Books.

Farreras, I. G. (2017). History of mental illness. In R. Biswas-Diener & E. Diener (Eds), Noba textbook series: Psychology. Champaign, IL: DEF publishers. DOI: nobaproject.com

Ferngren, G. B. (2014). Medicine and Religion: A historical introduction. Baltimore, Maryland: John Hopkins University Press.

Feist, G. & Rosenberg E. (2014). Psychology: Perspectives and connections. New York, New York: McGraw Hill Education.

Frankenburg, F. R. (2017). Medscape. Schizophrenia. Retrieved from http:emedicine.medscape.com.

Glass, A. (Director), Baldwin, D. Baraka, R., Chase, L., Eubanks, D., Franck, L., Neal, K., Seppelfrick, J., & Tomosunas, E. (Producers). 2016. The Secret She Kept (Television Movie). United States. Swirl Films.

Gorham, C. (2013). The Ebony Exodus Project: Why some black women are walking out on Religion---and others should too. Pitchstone Publishing.

Grob, G. N. (2014). From Asylum to Community: Mental health policy in Modern America. Princeton, New Jersey: Princeton University Press.

Hall, L. L. (2013). Genetics and mental illness: Evolving issues for research and society. New York, New York: Springer Science+Business Media.

Hankerson, S. H., Lee, Y. A., Brawley, D.K., Braswell, K., Wickramaratne, P. J. & Weissman, M.M. (2015). Screening for Depression in African-American Churches. National Institute of Health: Vol 49:526-533.

Hays, D. G. & Singh, A. A. (2012). Qualitative research Paradigms and traditions. In D. G. Hays & A. A. Singh (Eds.), Qualitative Inquiry in Clinical and Educational Settings (pp. 32-66). New York: The Guilford Press.

Islam, F. & Campbell, R. A. (2014). "Satan has afflicted me!" Jinn-Possession and Mental Illness in the Qur'an. Journal of Religion and Mental Health, Vol. 53(1): pp. 229-243. DOI:10.1007/s10943-012-9626-5

Keller, T. (2010). Four Models of Counseling in Pastoral Ministry. Redeemer City to City. Retrieved from www.nlch.org

Kemp, J. J., Lickel, J. J., & Deacon, B. J. (2014). Effects of a chemical imbalance causal explanation on individuals' perceptions of their depressive symptoms. Behaviour Research and Therapy, Vol. 56: pp. 47-52.

Kors, C. & Peters, E. (2001). Witchcraft in Europe, 400-1700: A documentary history. Philadelphia, Pennsylvania: University of Pennsylvania Press.

La Vista Church of Christ. (2016). Retrieved from lavistachurchofchrist.org

Laerd Dissertation. (2012). Research Strategy: Purposive Sampling. Retrieved from http://dissertation.laerd.com

Levine, L. E. & Munsch, J. (2014). Child development: an active learning approach. Second Edition. Thousand Oaks, California: SAGE.

Markway, B. & Markway, G. (2015). Painfully Shy: How to overcome social anxiety and reclaim your life. St. Martins Griffin, New York: Thomas Dunne Books.

McCammon, B. (2017). Semi-structured interviews. Design Research Techniques. Retrieved from http://designresearchtechniques.com

Medicinenet.com. (2017). Mental Illness. Retrieved from www.medicinenet.com

Mengesha, M. & Ward, E. C. (2012). Psychotherapy with African-American Women and Depression: Is it okay to talk about their religious/spiritual beliefs? Religions. Retrieved from www.mdpi.com/journal/religions

Mental Health Grace Alliance. (2014). How to get your church involved with Mental Illness Support. Retrieved from mentalhealthgracealliance.org

Merriam, S.B. (2009). Qualitative research: A guide to design and implementation. San Francisco, CA: Jossey-Bass.

Merriam Webster Dictionary. (2016). Definition of Mental Health. Retrieved from https://www.merriam-webster.com/dictionary/mental%20health

MindTools. (2017). Role Playing: Preparing for difficult conversations and situations. Retrieved from mindtools.com

Morrison-Valfre, M. (2017). Foundations of Mental Health Care. Sixth Edition. St. Louis, Missouri: Elsevier.

National Alliance on Mental Illness. (2017). Mental Health Statistics. Retrieved from http://www.nami.org/Learn-More/Mental-Health-By-the-Numbers

Newlife. (2017). Hidden Hurts. Retrieved from newlife.com

Newsweek. (2014). Nearly 1 in 5 Americans suffer from mental illness each year. Retrieved from newsweek.com

Olfson, M., Blanco, C., Wang, S. Laje, G. & Correll, C. (2014). National trends in the Mental Health Care of children, adolescents, and adults by office-based physicians. JAMA Psychiatry, 7(1): 81-90.

Parr, R. (Director), Eubanks, D., Tomosunas, E., & Aronson, S. (Producers). (2012). The Undershepherd (Television Movie). United States. Melee Entertainment.

Pell Institute. (2017). Evaluation Guide: Analyze Qualitative Data. Retrieved from http://toolkit.pellinstitute.org

Pellegrini, R. J. (2010). Identities for life and death: Can you save us from our toxically storied selves. Bloomington, Indiana: Author-house.

Perkins, Z. (2013). 5 Uncomfortable issues the church needs to talk about; Tearing down a few taboos in the body of Christ. Relevant. Retrieved from relevantmagazine.com

Pew Research Center. (2009). A religious portrait of African Americans. Religion and Public Life. Retrieved from pewforum.com

Rainer, S. (2015). Pastors, Counseling, and Mental Health: 6 Guidelines for Pastors to Consider. Retrieved from http://www.christianitytoday.com

Santrock, J. W. (2013). Life-Span Development. New York, NY: McGraw Hill Companies.

Sheffield, W. (2016). The Community Mental Health Act of 1963. Still pursuing the promise of reform fifty years later. Retrieved from https://www.ymadvocacy.org/the-community-mental-health-act-of-1963/

Shenton, A.K. (2004). Strategies for ensuring trustworthiness in qualitative research projects. Retrieved from http://www.crec.co.uk/docs/Trustworthypaper.pdf.

Simon, M. (n.d.). The role of the researcher. Retrieved from http://dissertationrecipes.com/wp-content/uploads/2011/04/Role-of-the-Researcher.pdf

Slate, R.N., Buffington-Vollum, J. K., & Johnson, W. W. (2013). The Criminalization of Mental Illness: Crisis and Opportunity for the Justice System. Durham, North Carolina: Carolina Academic Press.

Smith, G. & Hawes, J. B. (2017). Unsealed documents shed light on Dylan Roof's mental health issues. The Post and Courier. Retrieved from postandcourier.com

Stetzer, E. (2013). Mental Illness & Medication versus Spiritual Struggles & Biblical Counseling. Christianity Today. Retrieved from www.christianitytoday.com

Turner, L. O. (2017). How God can use your anxiety for good. Christian Today. Retrieved from christiantoday.com

Unite for Sight. (2015). Module 2: A brief history of mental illness and the U. S. Mental Health Care System. Retrieved from http://www.uniteforsight.org/mental-health/module2

United States Department of Health & Human Services. (2016). What is Mental Health? Retrieved from https://www.mentalhealth.gov/basics/what-is-mental-health/

University of Virginia. (2017). Retention of research records and destruction of data. Institutional Review Board for Social and Behavioral Sciences. Retrieved from www.virginia.edu

Veale, D. & Roberts, A. (2014). Obsessive Compulsive Disorder. Clinical Review, Vol. 348. doi: 10.1136/bmj.g2183

Wikidiff. (2017). The Difference-Between. Retrieved from http://wikidiff.com/spiritual/mental

Winfrey, O. (Director) & Virgo, C. (Producer). 2016. Greenleaf (Television Series). United States. Lionsgate Television.

World Health Organization. (2014). Mental Health: a state of well-being. Retrieved from http://www.who.int/features/factfiles/mental_health/en/

Young, M. D. (2010). Madness: An American History of mental illness and its treatment. Jefferson, North Carolina: McFarland & Company, Inc.

www.ingramcontent.com/pod-product-compliance
Lightning Source LLC
Chambersburg PA
CBHW031200160426
43193CB00008B/448